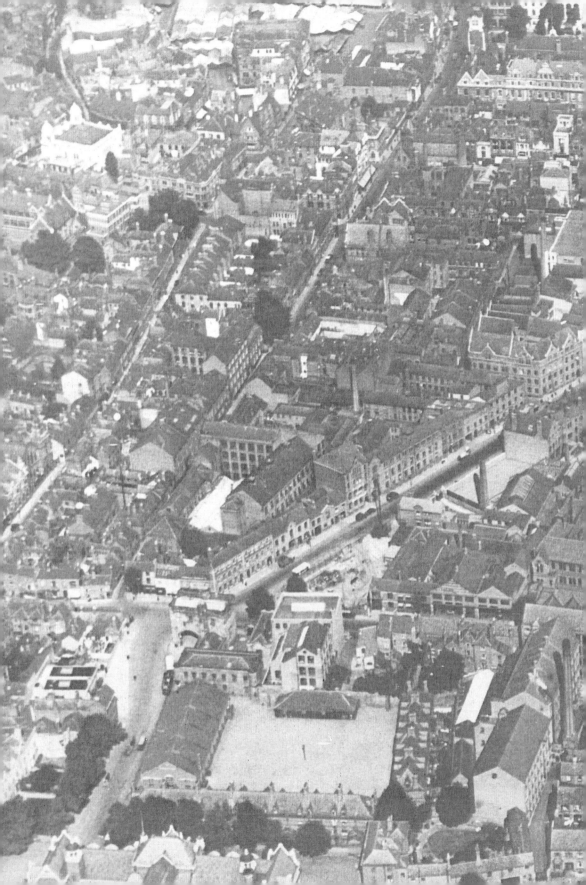

A CENTURY OF
LEICESTER

At this time, September 1903, Leicester's Clock Tower was said to preside over the most complicated tram junction in the country. Here Leicester Tramways Department's army of labourers conduct what became known as the 'siege' of the Clock Tower in preparation for electrification the following year. *(ROLLR)*

A CENTURY OF
LEICESTER

JESS & ROBIN JENKINS

First published in 2000 by Sutton Publishing Limited

This new paperback edition first published in 2007 by Sutton Publishing

Reprinted in 2011 by
The History Press
The Mill, Brimscombe Port,
Stroud, Gloucestershire, GL5 2QG
www.thehistorypress.co.uk

Reprinted 2013

British Library Cataloguing in Publication Data
A catalogue record for this book is available from the British Library.

ISBN 978-0-7509-4918-7

Front endpaper: A bird's-eye view of Leicester between the two world wars. The Magazine Gateway is clearly visible towards the bottom left, still with its associated militia buildings and parade ground. Two electric trams have just turned into Welford Road, while the old Parr's Bank building of 1900 shows up as a white mass on St Martin's. *(ROLLR)*
Back endpaper: A view of the Haymarket and Humberstone Gate at the end of the twentieth century. *(Authors)*
Half title page: Here tram number 149 turns out of Bowling Green Street. *(ROLLR)*
Title page: The Shires Shopping Centre, which opened in 1991: an interior view dominated by the grand staircase and glass lift. *(Authors)*

To our Leicester boys,
Sam and Thomas

Typeset in Photina.
Typesetting and origination by
Sutton Publishing.
Printed and bound in Great Britain by
Marston Book Services Limited, Didcot

Contents

The Family Fry Pan, William Hallam's shop on the corner of High Street and Highcross Street immediately prior to its demolition in 1903. When the building did come down, new premises were already prepared and stocked for business next door. Bold notices proclaimed it the 'Cheapest House in Leicester for Everything Useful'. *(ROLLR)*

Britain: A Century
of Change

Churchill in RAF uniform giving his famous victory sign, 1948.
(Illustrated London News)

The sixty years ending in 1900 were a period of huge transformation for Britain. Railway stations, post-and-telegraph offices, police and fire stations, gasworks and gasometers, new livestock markets and covered markets, schools, churches, football grounds, hospitals and asylums, water pumping stations and sewerage plants totally altered the urban scene, and the country's population tripled with more than seven out of ten people being born in or moving to the towns. The century that followed, leading up to the Millennium's end in 2000, was to be a period of even greater change.

When Queen Victoria died in 1901, she was measured for her coffin by her grandson Kaiser Wilhelm, the London prostitutes put on black mourning and the blinds came down in the villas and terraces spreading out from the old town centres. These centres were reachable by train and tram, by the new bicycles and still newer motor cars, were connected by the new telephone, and lit by gas or even electricity. The shops may have been full of British-made cotton and woollen clothing but the grocers and butchers were selling cheap Danish bacon, Argentinian beef, Australasian mutton and tinned or dried fish and fruit from Canada, California and South Africa. Most of these goods were carried in British-built-and-crewed ships burning Welsh steam coal.

Crowds celebrate Armistice Day outside Buckingham Palace as the royal family appears on the balcony, 1918. (*Illustrated London News*)

As the first decade moved on, the Open Spaces Act meant more parks, bowling greens and cricket pitches. The First World War transformed the place of women, as they took over many men's jobs. Its other legacies were the war memorials which joined the statues of Victorian worthies in main squares round the land. After 1918 death duties and higher taxation bit hard, and a quarter of England changed hands in the space of only a few years.

The multiple shop – the chain store – appeared in the high street: Marks & Spencer, Sainsburys, Maypole, Lipton's, Home & Colonial, the Fifty Shilling Tailor, Burton, Boots, W.H. Smith. The shopper was spoilt for choice, attracted by the brash fascias and advertising hoardings for national brands like Bovril, Pears Soap, and Ovaltine. Many new buildings began to be seen, such as garages, motor showrooms, picture palaces (cinemas), 'palais de dance', and ribbons of 'semis' stretched along the roads and new bypasses and onto the new estates nudging the green belts.

During the 1920s cars became more reliable and sophisticated as well as commonplace, with developments like the electric self-starter making them easier for women to drive. Who wanted to turn a crank handle in the new short skirt? This was, indeed, the electric age as much as the motor era. Trolley buses, electric trams and trains extended mass transport and electric light replaced gas in the street and the home, which itself was groomed by the vacuum cleaner.

A major jolt to the march onward and upward was administered by the Great Depression of the early 1930s. The older British industries – textiles, shipbuilding, iron, steel, coal – were already under pressure from foreign competition when this worldwide slump arrived. Luckily there were new diversions to alleviate the misery. The 'talkies' arrived in the cinemas; more and more radios and gramophones were to be found in people's homes; there were new women's magazines, with fashion, cookery tips and problem pages; football pools; the flying feats of women pilots like Amy Johnson; the Loch Ness Monster; cheap chocolate and the drama of Edward VIII's abdication.

Houghton of Aston Villa beats goalkeeper Crawford of Blackburn to score the second of four goals, 1930s. *(Illustrated London News)*

Things were looking up again by 1936 and new light industry was booming in the Home Counties as factories struggled to keep up with the demand for radios, radiograms, cars and electronic goods, including the first television sets. The threat from Hitler's Germany meant rearmament, particularly of the airforce, which stimulated aircraft and aero engine firms. If you were lucky and lived in the south, there was good money to be earned. A semi-detached house cost £450, a Morris Cowley £150. People may have smoked like chimneys but life expectancy, since 1918, was up by 15 years while the birth rate had almost halved.

In some ways it is the little memories that seem to linger longest from the Second World War: the kerbs painted white to show up in the blackout, the rattle of ack-ack shrapnel on roof tiles, sparrows killed by bomb blast. The biggest damage, apart from London, was in the south-west (Plymouth, Bristol) and the Midlands (Coventry, Birmingham). Postwar reconstruction was rooted in the Beveridge Report which set out the expectations for the Welfare State. This, together with the nationalisation of the Bank of England, coal, gas, electricity and the railways, formed the programme of the Labour government in 1945.

Times were hard in the late 1940s, with rationing even more stringent than during the war. Yet this was, as has been said, 'an innocent and well-behaved era'. The first let-up came in 1951 with the Festival of Britain and there was another fillip in 1953 from the Coronation, which incidentally gave a huge boost to the spread of TV. By 1954 leisure motoring had been resumed but the Comet – Britain's best hope for taking on the American aviation industry – suffered a series of mysterious crashes. The Suez debacle of 1956 was followed by an acceleration in the withdrawal from Empire, which had begun in 1947 with the Independence of India. Consumerism was truly born with the advent of commercial TV and most homes soon boasted washing machines, fridges, electric irons and fires.

WAAF personnel tracing the movement of flying bombs and Allied fighters on a plotting table, 1944. *(Illustrated London News)*

The *Lady Chatterley* obscenity trial in 1960 was something of a straw in the wind for what was to follow in that decade. A collective loss of inhibition seemed to sweep the land, as the Beatles and the Rolling Stones transformed popular music, and retailing, cinema and the theatre were revolutionised. Designers, hairdressers, photo-graphers and models moved into places vacated by an Establishment put to flight by the new breed of satirists spawned by *Beyond the Fringe* and *Private Eye*.

In the 1970s Britain seems to have suffered a prolonged hangover after the excesses of the previous decade. Ulster, inflation and union troubles were not made up for by entry into the EEC, North Sea Oil, Women's Lib or, indeed, Punk Rock. Mrs Thatcher applied the corrective in the 1980s, as the country moved over more and more from its old manufacturing base to providing services, consulting, advertising, and expertise in the 'invisible' market of high finance or in IT.

The post-1945 townscape has seen changes to match those in the worlds of work, entertainment and politics. In 1952 the Clean Air Act served notice on smogs and pea-souper fogs, smuts and blackened buildings, forcing people to stop burning coal and go over to smokeless sources of heat and energy. In the same decade some of the best urban building took place in the 'new towns' like Basildon, Crawley, Stevenage and Harlow. Elsewhere open warfare was declared on slums and what was labelled inadequate, cramped, back-to-back, two-up, two-down, housing. The new 'machine for living in' was a flat in a high-rise block. The architects and planners who promoted these were in league with the traffic engineers, determined to keep the motor car moving whatever the price in multi-storey car parks, meters, traffic wardens and ring roads. The old pollutant, coal smoke, was replaced by petrol and diesel exhaust, and traffic noise.

Fast food was no longer only a pork pie in a pub or fish-and-chips. There were Indian curry houses, Chinese take-aways and American-style hamburgers, while the drinker could get away from beer in a wine bar. Under the impact of television the big Gaumonts and Odeons closed or were rebuilt as multi-screen cinemas, while the palais de dance gave way to discos and clubs.

From the late 1960s the introduction of listed buildings and conservation areas, together with the growth of preservation societies, put a brake on 'comprehensive redevelopment'. The end of the century and the start of the Third Millennium saw new challenges to the health of towns and the wellbeing of the nine out of ten people who now live urban lives. The fight is on to prevent town centres from dying, as patterns of housing and shopping change, and edge-of-town supermarkets exercise the attractions of one-stop shopping. But as banks and department stores close, following the haberdashers, greengrocers, butchers and ironmongers, there are signs of new growth such as farmers' markets, and corner stores acting as pick-up points where customers collect shopping ordered on-line from web sites.

Futurologists tell us that we are in stage two of the consumer revolution: a shift from mass consumption to mass customisation driven by a desire to have things that fit us and our particular lifestyle exactly, and for better service. This must offer hope for small city-centre shop premises, as must the continued attraction of physical shopping, browsing and being part of a crowd: in a word, 'shoppertainment'. Another hopeful trend for towns is the growth in the number of young

11

Manchester during the Commonwealth Games in 2002. The city, like others all over the country, has experienced massive redevelopment and rejuvenation in recent years. *(Chris Makepeace)*

people postponing marriage and looking to live independently, alone, where there is a buzz, in 'swinging single cities'. Theirs is a 'flats-and-cafés' lifestyle, in contrast to the 'family suburbs', and certainly fits in with government's aim of building 60 per cent of the huge amount of new housing needed on 'brown' sites, recycled urban land. There looks to be plenty of life in the British town yet.

Leicester: An Introduction

Leicester at the beginning of the twentieth century was a bustling, prosperous place, 'one of the brightest and *best kept* of manufacturing towns', as the 1912 *Little Guide* put it. The town was thriving too, both economically and in terms of population. In the fifty years from 1851 to 1901 the number of Leicester's inhabitants rose from just over 60,000 to 174,624. The rise was partly due to the borough's expansion into surrounding areas but in the main it was the rising birth-rate, healthier living and economic migration.

Without a doubt the period from the death of Queen Victoria to the outbreak of the First World War was one of progress in Leicester. The Corporation continued to improve provision of the necessities of life: clean water, lighting, removal of sewage and waste, and good communications. Inhabitants of the borough also enjoyed good schools, theatres and other places of entertainment, parks and sporting venues, libraries, a museum, and a variety of churches and chapels. The borough was remarkably well behaved too: on three occasions in 1906 the assize judges were presented with the white gloves that symbolised an empty calendar of prisoners – no cases to try.

A modern view of Leicester Market Place, seen through its gateway which is decorated with symbols of the goods available within. Dominating the market stalls is the Corn Exchange, built between 1850 and 1855. *(Authors)*

Leicester was changing, however. From 1898 the Corporation had been buying up property along the High Street and in 1902 demolition began, to accommodate the double track of the new electric trams. Faster travel on the efficient new network led to ever more development at the edges of the town and Leicester's new suburbs, Aylestone, Belgrave, Knighton, Humberstone and Evington, blossomed.

Leicester's industry began to move out from the centre too. In 1911 the manufacture of footwear, employing 23,495 directly and many more in allied trades, was pre-eminent. Most women,-however, worked in the hosiery trade, which employed some 6,162 of Leicester's workers.

Such trades knew slumps as well as booms, as the Unemployed Marchers of 1905 had so eloquently demonstrated, but as war loomed in August 1914 Leicester was 'doing well'.

The First World War brought the period of progress to an end. At first events on the continent seemed rather remote. Reservists departed and Belgian refugees came. The Base Hospital was established in the old lunatic asylum and appeals were issued for private motor vehicles, for beds, and above all for recruits. Leicester did not at first, however, answer the call. Perhaps it was the temporary boom in the town's principal trades that kept its young men at their benches and out of khaki. Certainly many of Leicester's political leaders, including one of the MPs, J. Ramsay MacDonald, were hesitant in their support for the war.

The sewing room at Adderly's Department Store, Market Place, *c.* 1900. Adderly's was for a long time regarded as one of the city's leading stores. *(ROLLR)*

Total war, however, exempts no-one, and Leicester mobilised. The town's men were again appealed to and the Town Hall was cloaked in recruiting posters. In the end some 9,348 local men gave their lives and thousands more were wounded. Conscription ended the need for recruitment drives, while Leicester's women were also called upon to fill the places of absent men. The town's factories, many converted to munition or other war-work, were kept running by women, as were the trams, post office, railways and hospitals.

The postwar world into which Leicester emerged in 1918 was a different place to that which had gone before. In 1919 Leicester had at last become a city, achieving again a status lost in the ninth century and for which it had unsuccessfully petitioned in 1889 and 1891 and which its nearby rival, Nottingham, had gained in 1897. In 1921 the new city acquired a college of higher education on the site of the lunatic asylum (and wartime hospital), which in 1926 became Leicester University College.

In 1920 unemployment began to reappear in Leicester's staple industries. By mid-1931 the number of those out of work, which had risen constantly, reached a total of 16,225, with perhaps another 12,000 on short-time, in a total population of 229,000. Even so, the town never suffered as badly as most of Britain's other industrial centres and the general economic trend in Leicester was one of growth.

Growth characterised the city physically too in the inter-war period. Successive Housing Acts, in 1919 and 1923, allowed the City Council to acquire land and to build new estates around the city boundaries in North Evington, West Humberstone and in 1925 Braunstone and Saffron Lane. In the decade after the end of the war the City Council had built well over 4,000 houses. In the following ten years some 4,600 more were built, though the emphasis increasingly became one of slum clearance allied to urban redevelopment as traffic became increasingly heavy and more congested.

The onset of war in 1939 brought a temporary halt to slum clearance and improvement schemes. For the next five years at least, the attention of Leicester's citizens was turned to national events. Fortunately the city was to escape the worst of the bombing raids inflicted upon other Midlands cities like Birmingham and Coventry, although its own experience was quite enough to convince the inhabitants of the horrors of this new aspect of total war. On the night of 19 November 1940 around thirty aircraft attacked the city in a raid which lasted from 7.40 p.m. to 1.30 a.m. The terrible loss of life aside, it left 2,855 houses destroyed, 56 industrial premises gutted and 8,000 houses damaged. In all the city was to suffer eight raids, although no other was to match the destruction of that terrible night.

The Castle Gateway, *c.* 1920. In front of the fifteenth-century gatehouse and the Norman doorway of St Mary de Castro is a German field gun. Such trophies of the Great War were, for a time, common sights about the country. Children, at least, found them attractive playthings. *(ROLLR)*

It is a joke common to many modern cities, including Leicester, that the city planners finished off the work which the Luftwaffe had started. First, however, the most pressing problem following the end of the war was that posed by a lack of houses. Between 1945 and 1954 Leicester City Council constructed over 8,000 council houses in a bid to address the need. By 1955 economic conditions had improved to the extent that the slum clearance programme could be renewed and a large area was cleared in St Margaret's parish, next to the district cleared in the 1930s. New residential areas just outside the city boundary also sprang up.

Leicester at this time was still a flourishing industrial centre, with some 28,000 employed in the manufacture of hosiery and 27,000 in engineering and metal-working. The boot and shoe industry, which employed around 18,000 workers, had by then lost its predominance – perhaps a sign, for the more thoughtful, of things to come.

A significant building programme had commenced on the site of the old University College, which had achieved university status in 1957 – in particular the modern tower block of the Engineering Building, built between 1959 and 1963, which was to attract much critical acclaim. Amidst this atmosphere of growing confidence Leicester City established its first separate planning department in 1962. It was then that the planners set about redesigning Leicester with a complete disregard for the town's former glories, and leaving its medieval street pattern shattered. In tackling the long suffered problem of traffic congestion in the narrow streets of the old town, the planners were to introduce a series of dramatic road schemes which sacrificed everything to the dominance of the motor vehicle and paid little heed to the considerations of historical value and environmental needs which only a few decades later were

to be recognised as of vital importance. This is not the place to dwell upon the sad list of architectural losses incurred at this time; the photographs will speak for themselves.

There were other changes in Leicester at this time, although few could have foreseen their lasting significance. Leicester had long attracted migrants because of the varied nature of the employment offered and over the years it had welcomed many different nationalities, all of whom had contributed to the town's success and prosperity. By the late 1950s more and more immigrants from the Indian sub-continent – particularly the regions of Gujerat and Punjab – had chosen to settle in Leicester. From 1968 their numbers were also swollen by many thousands of Asians who had been forced to leave Africa. The ethnically diverse communities which grew up in Leicester as a result have been tremendously successful, often breathing new life into previously moribund areas. The most famous example of this process is 'the Golden Mile' of the Belgrave and Melton Roads, which with its numerous jewellers, ethnic goods and food stores and colourful sari shops continues to attract visitors from a wide area, particularly during Diwali celebrations. Such changes have left many lasting marks on the architecture of the city, with the appearance of mosques and the conversion of several former church and chapel properties for use as temples for the Hindu faithful and others. Leicester continues to benefit enormously from the rich cultural diversity and vitality which has been introduced into city life.

In the recessions of the 1980s the loss of much of Leicester's industrial base resulted in considerable adjustments in the city's

Gwendolen Road sweeps around to the south of The Circle in this aerial view of the Crown Hills development from 1932. Traces of the medieval ridge and furrow are still just visible in the fields round about. (ROLLR)

economy. As elsewhere service industries assumed a far more important role and Leicester's importance as a shopping and entertainment centre became all the more significant. Redevelopment schemes now turned towards creating attractive pedestrianised streets and squares, with the emphasis on enhancing the shopper's experience in a traffic-free environment. Guidebooks stressed words like 'traditional', 'unique' and 'intimate' which would have astonished the planners of the 1960s.

Another piece of old Leicester about to disappear for ever. The corner shop on Bradgate Street and Abbey Gate forlornly awaits demolition in December 1963. *(ROLLR)*

The latest of these developments was the opening of the prestigious Shires Shopping Centre in 1991, which succeeded in combining sensitivity with innovation. At the end of the century the increased emphasis upon refurbishment of old buildings and regeneration of urban areas seemed to display a new understanding of what added quality to life. None the less the continuing preoccupation with efforts to discourage cars from the centre of Leicester suggested that some problems at least were still to be tackled.

In the 1990s Leicester could be justly proud of itself as a successful, multi-cultural city. It enjoyed the prestige of having two well-regarded

universities, the De Montfort Hall and Haymarket Theatre, and of being home to the Leicester City Football Club, the 'Tigers' rugby club and Leicestershire County Cricket Club; all champions in their respective sports.

Silver linings do not come without clouds, however, and Leicester was not without its problems. The City Council achieved unitary status when local government was reformed in 1997, which brought extra burdens of responsibility as well as opportunities. As the twentieth century slipped away Leicester's schools, libraries and museums all faced cuts in their budgets, and question marks hung over the Granby Halls and Haymarket Theatre.

Leicester has faced problems just as great as these before, though, and triumphed. What will the twenty-first century bring?

The photographs in this book can only tell a small part of the story of the people and events which helped to shape Leicester in the twentieth century. It is hoped that this photographic record will give a taste of life in Leicester over those 100 years.

An interesting survival of old Leicester, seen in the last year of the twentieth century. A view from Guildhall Lane down Silver Street, showing the twisting of the medieval street pattern. (*Authors*)

A Bustling Town

A policeman on point duty watches calmly as a horse tram weaves among the traffic of Horsefair Street. The clock tower of the Town Hall looms through the early morning mist, *c.* 1902. *(ROLLR)*

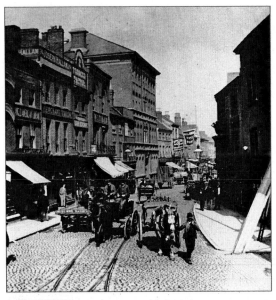

A busy street scene at the point where the Haymarket becomes Belgrave Gate, *c.* 1902. A satisfied customer leaves the doorway of the tailor and outfitter, Joseph Hallam, which nestles between the offices of the Anglo American Nitrogen Company and the pawnbroker's establishment of Edward Wilham at 4 Belgrave Gate. *(ROLLR)*

Below: A mid-morning crush of horse buses, trams, carts and cabs at the Clock Tower in the first or second year of the twentieth century. The shoppers might buy boots from Freeman Hardy & Willis, tea from Francis Broomhall or a new suit from Wacks Brothers. *(ROLLR)*

Above: A crowded horse bus passes the Huntingdon Tower on the High Street. The tower, the last remnant of The Lord's Place, the town house of the Earl of Huntingdon, was a witness to many of Leicester's historic events. In November 1569 the Earl briefly became host there to the imprisoned Mary, Queen of Scots on her way from Tutbury, via Ashby de la Zouch, to Coventry. *(ROLLR)*

A last glimpse of the Huntingdon Tower on 3 May 1902, the day it was finally demolished. The tower was one of many casualties as the High Street was widened to accommodate double tramlines. *(ROLLR)*

21

Laying tramlines in London Road, 1903.
The change from horse-drawn to electric
trams was to involve the laying of 20 miles of
track and 40 miles of overhead copper wire.
Leicester's electric trams were to remain in
operation for some forty-five years, travelling
in the course of their work nearly 172 million
miles! *(ROLLR)*

Above: The Belgrave Road station of the Great Northern Railway, *c.* 1902. The station-master of the passenger station in 1902 was a Stephen Bee, while William Goodship managed the goods station. The station had opened in October 1882 and was to close to passenger traffic in 1957. It closed fully in 1962. *(ROLLR)*

The top-hatted Mayor and aldermen of Leicester pass the Clock Tower, on the morning of 18 May 1904, aboard the last of the town's horse-drawn trams. The Mayor, Stephen Hilton, was born in the town in 1845. He was a boot manufacturer and had represented the Liberal interest on the town council since 1894. Beside him is his wife, Harriet Gibson. A fleet of twelve horse trams carried the mayor and 300 guests to Painter Street where, at the Corporate power station, the electricity was switched on for the new trams. The party then travelled to the terminuses at Belgrave and Stoneygate by open-topped electric tram, before a public service, free for the evening, began from the Clock Tower. *(ROLLR)*

The opening ceremony for the Leicester electric trams at their Stoneygate terminus, 18 May 1904. The Leicester Tramways Company had first opened a horse-drawn tramway in 1874, but it was only when the Leicester Corporation purchased the undertaking in 1901 that a new system of electric tramways was finally adopted. *(ROLLR)*

A view from Gallowtree Gate of the last great fair to be held in Humberstone Gate, May 1904. Although it began as a cheesefair held in the Market Place on 13 May each year, the funfair spilled out and down Humberstone Gate. Biscuits and confectionery are on sale from the stalls, and the canopy of a merry-go-round is just visible in the distance. *(ROLLR)*

Boys will be boys – as this view of youthful mischief in Church Gate, *c.* 1900, confirms. *(ROLLR)*

The Reverend James Went, headmaster of Wyggeston Boys' School, gets carried away with enthusiasm at a prize giving – possibly the annual Infirmary Sports at Aylestone Road sports ground. Canon Went had been appointed headmaster in 1877 and stayed in post until 1919. After retirement he remained a notable figure in Leicester society, being appointed an honorary freeman in 1925. He died a few days before his ninety-first birthday on 10 March 1936. *(ROLLR)*

A keenly observed doubles match on the playing fields of the Wyggeston Girls' School, *c.* 1910. In the background is the long building of Wyggeston's Hospital which had been built in 1869, only to be demolished in 1966. *(ROLLR)*

At the final of the Midlands County Cup Competition, held at Coventry on 1 April 1905, the Tigers succeeded in retaining the trophy for a record eighth time and in so doing imposed the greatest defeat ever in a final on their Nottingham opponents, winning 31–0. They were to be welcomed back in triumph with crowds lining London Road. *(ROLLR)*

Ladies' Day at the Victoria Park Bowling Club, June 1909. Mrs Matthews, closely observed by Councillor Joseph Collier, sporting a jolly button–hole, lets fly with a game-winning throw. *(ROLLR)*

Waiters, doormen and housekeeper pose for a group photograph at the Manchester Club, 39 Humberstone Gate, 1913. The Club was established for members of registered friendly societies and by 1914 had around 900 members, each paying 6½*d* a month for the privilege. Concerts – hence the stage at the back – were held on three days a week and other attractions included a miniature rifle range, skittles and billiards. The Club still existed in 1970 when it was known as the Manchester Working Men's Club. *(ROLLR)*

Two trams pass in Horsefair Street in front
of Atlas House, the main outlet of
T. Inglesant & Sons Ltd, cabinet makers
and upholsterers, house furnishers and
removers, *c.* 1905. *(ROLLR)*

31

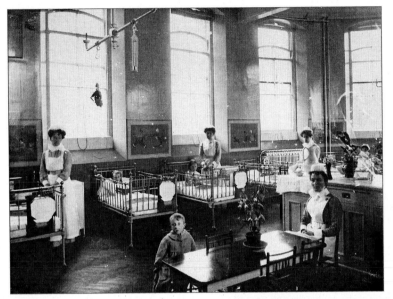

A ward in the Royal Infirmary's Children's Hospital, *c.* 1905. The Infirmary was founded, after much prompting, by Dr William Watts of Danet's Hall, in 1768. The building was completed by 1771 but had to wait until 1889 for its Children's Hospital. Here are five of its forty-two cots. Scarcely a toy in sight! *(ROLLR)*

Below: A congenial atmosphere in one of the Royal Infirmary's wards, *c.* 1905. The potted plants and domestic furniture create a homely feeling and the attentive staff, apparently far outnumbering patients, suggest a concern for patient welfare, albeit rather regimented. *(ROLLR)*

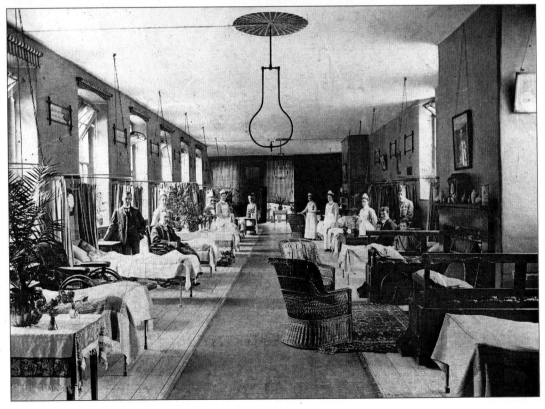

George White, Secretary of the Unemployed Committee, with representatives of the 400 unemployed who marched with him to London in June 1905 to protest to the King about conditions suffered by Leicester's some 2,000 unemployed and their families. In the event the King refused to meet them but the marchers did succeed in winning much sympathy. The money collected on the march was used to alleviate conditions at home. This march and others like it must have influenced the government, and helped to hasten the introduction of the Unemployed Workmen Act which first granted state assistance to the unemployed. *(ROLLR)*

Members of the hunger march halt for refreshments somewhere between Leicester and London during their week-long march. Overnight the men usually stayed in schoolrooms and chapel accommodation. The weather was not always kind and the final rally planned in Hyde Park had to be cancelled because of the rain. Instead a final meeting was held in Trafalgar Square addressed by members of the Labour Party, before the marchers returned to Leicester. Each marcher received a commemorative medal for his pains. *(ROLLR)*

A cartoonist's view of the congestion at the Clock Tower after electrification of the trams. In the newspapers Leicester Corporation Tramways boasted proudly of the number of passengers it conveyed each week. In the week ending 1 April 1905 the trams had carried a total of 462,208 people, of whom by far the largest number – 113,835 – had travelled on the Saturday. *(ROLLR)*

Two of Leicester Corporation's electric trams, already accepted and unnoticed, after a couple of months' service in 1904. Beneath a huge 'Twice Nightly' at the Palace Theatre of Varieties, nestle the shops of William Henry Newman, the tobacconist, and Edward Kemp, the watchmaker. *(ROLLR)*

Having swilled down Rutland Street, the Corporation's water cart pauses at the junction with Humberstone Road – opposite a branch of the Leicester Coffee & Cocoa House Company. The streets of Edwardian Leicester may have been free of the litter that clogs ours but the dust of poor road surfaces and the many horses employed created a need for cleansing. *(ROLLR)*

Doing its bit to keep the streets clean, the Post Office bought its first motor van into operation in December 1910. In Leicester the Postmaster, Mr Edward J.E. Bovill, with a staff of 143 sorting clerks and supervisors and 228 postmen, could offer no fewer than six deliveries in the town and collections up until late morning for same-day delivery as far afield as Liverpool, Manchester, Glasgow and London. *(ROLLR)*

Staff at work in the blind making and fitting workshop of R. Morley & Son of 28 Market Place and 30 Cank Street. In a 1902 trade directory they were described as complete house furnishers 'established over 70 years'. Employees who lived in were said to belong to one big happy family, despite the odd restriction such as attendance at church every Sunday. *(ROLLR)*

The linen department at Adderly's, *c.* 1910. Employees, who enjoyed the benefits of a good training scheme and a large hostel in Princess Street, were regarded as highly privileged. The store was later acquired by Marshall and Snelgrove. *(ROLLR)*

Opposite: A customer is served in the Ladies' Wear Department of Adderly's & Co. Ltd, Market Place, *c.* 1910. Alfred Adderly had founded a humble draper's business in 1856 but by 1900 he was director of an expanding company which prided itself as silk mercers, milliners, dress and mantle makers of the highest quality. *(ROLLR)*

Perhaps the model for the 'Laughing Policeman', Police Constable James William Stephens was by no means as inactive as his 23 stone figure might suggest. He served with the Royal Artillery in the Zulu War of 1879 and is seen here wearing his campaign medal. *(ROLLR)*

Below: The funeral procession of PC Stephens accompanied by 30 policemen, passing the prison en route to Welford Road Cemetery, 8 April 1908. Stephens' imposing figure was a familiar sight on point duty at the Clock Tower or in Belvoir Street for over twenty-two years. He died from heart disease and dropsy on 4 April. His coffin required eight policemen to lift it and had to be removed from his house in Cobden Street by way of the window. *(ROLLR)*

A Labour Party meeting at the Temperance Hall, Leicester, February 1911. J.R. Clyne addresses the audience on the subject of the Party's view of militarism, while on his left sits Keir Hardie, founder of the Labour Party. Ramsay MacDonald, Leicester's MP from 1906 until 1918, is seated in the front row, two seats to the speaker's right. Also visible behind MacDonald's left shoulder is the Revd F.L. Donaldson, one of the leaders of Leicester's Unemployed March of 1905. (ROLLR)

The girls from Thomas Brown & Co. Ltd ladies' shoe factory in Humberstone Road, c. 1912. Though apparently turned out in their 'Sunday best', the group is actually a trade union picket during a strike for shorter working hours. (ROLLR)

A smartly dressed Leicester
crowd enjoying one of the
series of band concerts
in Victoria Park, 1909.
The popularity of the
concerts encouraged
the Corporation's Parks
Committee to engage
such bands as those
of the 1st Life Guards
and Royal Marines from
Portsmouth. The Pavilion
in the background was
demolished after it received
a direct hit from a German
land mine in 1940.
(ROLLR)

A blacksmith is caught at work by the camera, *c.* 1905. The photograph is said to be of a wheelwright's shop in Arundel Street. The workers can have had little idea of how short a time there was left for horse-drawn transport. *(ROLLR)*

Although his wares obscure the name and half the street number of the shop, the three golden balls give the game away. This is the pawnbroker's shop of Alfred Whysall. Originally in Syston Street, the business moved early in the century to 182 Humberstone Road (where this photograph was taken) and remained there until the 1960s. *(ROLLR)*

A carnival float bearing local supporters of the Women's Social and Political Union for Votes for Women passes London Road station, *c.* 1914. Seated on the left is Eva Lines and to the right Violet West, both of Birstall. *(ROLLR)*

Below: Miss Grew addressing a predominantly masculine crowd on the virtues of emancipation for women. This was one of a series of meetings held in the Market Place in June 1913. Miss Grew's audience would appear to be attentive, if (in some quarters) a little sceptical. *(ROLLR)*

Forever caught in time as he dashed for the tram, a running youth is seen here in Granby Street, *c.* 1914. The closed gate and drawn blinds of Spencer and Greenhough's bookshop and the long shadows from the west suggest it is early evening, and that the tram is carrying Leicester's workers and shoppers home. *(ROLLR)*

They Did Not Fail Us

A kiss and a tickle from uncle's bristling moustache as a party of territorials from the
Leicestershire Regiment gather outside London Road station. The age of the soldiers and their
outdated equipment suggest that these are recently mobilised reservists, early in the
Great War. *(ROLLR)*

Captain Geoffrey
Codrington leads
'A' Squadron of the
Leicestershire Yeomanry
down Gallowtree Gate
in August 1914. The
regiment was on its way
to join the North Midland
Mounted Brigade
at Grantham. From
Grantham the Yeomanry
moved to Diss, in Norfolk,
and then across the
Channel to join the
British Expeditionary
Force in France. *(ROLLR)*

A draft for the 10th (Reserve) Battalion of the Leicestershire Regiment is seen off at London Road station by relatives and the band from the depot at Glen Parva. The battalion was stationed at Cannock Chase, Staffordshire. *(ROLLR)*

Opposite: Drumming up recruits at the Town Hall, May 1915. Recruitment was actually rather slow in Leicester throughout the first ten months of the war. Three Leicester recruits came forward for every eighteen who joined the colours in Nottingham and there was much scandalised talk of the town feeling the war to be none of its concern. In May 1915 a great drive for recruits, part of which was the conversion of two rooms at the Town Hall for recruitment, began to change the statistics. By the end of the war over 9,300 men of Leicester and Leicestershire had given their lives. *(ROLLR)*

The official opening of the cottage in Harvey Lane, where William Carey (1761–1834), missionary and founder of the Baptist Missionary Society, lived from 1789 to 1793. The new museum, housing relics relating to Carey's life, was opened by the Mayor, Alderman Jonathan North, on 22 September 1915. It is an interesting reflection of the changing values of the century that the cottage was demolished in 1968 to make way for redevelopment. *(ROLLR)*

Volunteers man a stall to raise funds to pay for food parcels for prisoners of war, in front of the South African War Memorial on Town Hall Square, in October 1915. The Revd Francis Payne, Vicar of St Margaret's church, had first been moved to commence fundraising a few months earlier when he had received a postcard from a soldier who asked simply that bread be sent to Germany for prisoners of war, since 'we cannot live without (it)'. The postcard was read out in church services around Leicester and from that start grew what was later to become the large and efficient organisation known as the Leicester, Leicestershire and Rutland Prisoner of War Committee. *(ROLLR)*

Below: The newest recruit to the 11th Battalion, Leicestershire Regiment, the 'Midland Pioneers', was a hungry little monkey, presented by Miss Flora Scott on 24 March 1916. The battalion had been raised by Leicester's Mayor, Jonathan North, in the autumn of 1915 and was sent to France shortly after this picture was taken. *(ROLLR)*

One of the 363 hospital trains received at Leicester during the Great War. The most seriously wounded soldiers were of course dealt with by hospitals in London or near to the point of disembarkation from France, but casualties who were unlikely to suffer from longer journeys were dispatched further inland. Here members of the Voluntary Aid Detachments and Royal Army Medical Corps unload a hospital train at London Road station. From the station a fleet of ambulances and private vehicles will convey them to the 5th Northern General Hospital. *(ROLLR)*

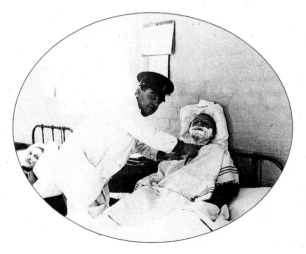

From a close shave with death, this patient at the 5th Northern General Hospital has moved to a close shave with the Royal Army Medical Corps. Neither patient nor barber seems concerned at the need to pause for the camera. *(ROLLR)*

Life at the Base Hospital had its compensations. On the outbreak of war, in August 1914, the Territorial Army's 5th Northern General Hospital returned from its annual 'camp' and occupied the old lunatic asylum buildings in Leicester (now the Leicester University site). The spacious grounds permitted all manner of outdoor pursuits – including the clock golf played here by a Gordon Highlander and his chums. *(ROLLR)*

A party of newly discharged patients from the 5th Northern General Hospital, the Base Hospital, awaiting transport, *c.* 1918. By the time the last patient departed, on 10 September 1919, some 74,652 soldiers (including 59 prisoners of war) had been treated. *(ROLLR)*

One of the many significant changes in life brought in by the First World War was the role women played, stepping into the shoes of male workers who had gone to the Front. Here a remarkably happy band of women clean the windows and paintwork of a carriage belonging to the Great Central Railway. The men present look rather more dubious about the situation. What has just been said? *(ROLLR)*

Another new and, to some, rather startling sight was the appearance of female ticket collectors on the Corporation trams and buses. Here a driver and a conductress (later Mrs A. Leeson) pose beside their number 19 tram, on East Park Road, *c.* 1916. In the early part of 1915 the Corporation had voted – against some opposition – for tram fares to be reduced by half for all men serving in the forces below commissioned rank. It was felt that the poor levels of pay justified the reduction. *(ROLLR)*

Members of the Women's Land Army parade through Leicester in an effort to encourage recruitment, on Women's Day, 17 April 1918. The Women's Land Army had first been organised in 1917 in answer to the great problems in agriculture caused by the loss of manpower. Despite lower wages than those received in other occupations and the isolation and discomfort of farm life, the girls proved themselves more than able to take on the roles previously reserved for men. Their success in achieving increased food production was not forgotten in 1939 when a Women's Land Army was formed immediately upon the outbreak of war. With the Land Army girls in the parade were also detachments of VADs and factory workers, who carried aeroplane parts to show the products of their efforts. They are just visible behind the Land Girls. *(ROLLR)*

A City Once More

A view of the Clock Tower, probably from the tower of Lewis's department store in Humberstone Gate, *c.* 1938. In the background is the chimney of the Fielding Johnson Ltd woollen mills in West Bond Street. *(ROLLR)*

The Town Clerk reads to assembled councillors the Royal Charter which made Leicester once again a city in 1919. During the war many had advocated the return of city status, which the town had last enjoyed in the ninth century. *(ROLLR)*

Amos Sherriff (1856–1945), Mayor of Leicester in 1922, stands flanked by members of the Salvation Army. Sherriff by his own admission had been 'born in a mean house in a mean street in Leicester' and had started work in a brickyard at the age of 6½ years. At twenty-two he was found weeping because he could not read or write, but at this stage of his life he joined the Salvation Army and his prospects were transformed. His service on behalf of Leicester's poor was to be tireless and in 1905 he was one of the leaders of the Unemployed March to London. Sherriff was elected to the town council in 1908 and was one of the foremost in arguing for the return of city status. *(ROLLR)*

On the evening of 5 July 1919 the murdered body of Bella Wright was found at Little Stretton, a few miles east of Leicester. The police sought a scruffy looking man on a green bicycle, who had been seen in her company earlier that day. The trail cooled, but on 23 February 1920 it suddenly became red hot when the rope of a narrow boat on the Soar Navigation snagged and fished up the frame of a green bicycle. The canal was dragged by the police, represented here by Sergeant Healey and Constables Bailey and Steele. More cycle parts, together with a holster and pistol ammunition were brought to the surface. The bicycle frame had a number. The number led to the maker's order book. The order book led to a shop in Derby and the shop to . . .

. . . Ronald Vivian Light. A Leicester man, born in Seymour Street in 1885, Light was also a rogue with a record of indecency and a dishonourable discharge from the army. He was arrested and tried for his life at Leicester Castle but acquitted on 11 June 1920. Light's unsavoury past was, of course, no concern of the jury and his barrister, Sir Edward Marshall Hall, conducted a brilliant defence. Light had the benefit of the doubt, but with modern forensic science he might not have been so lucky. This photograph was doctored for publication at the time.

The evening rush hour just beginning
at the London & North Eastern Railway
station in Great Central Street,
c. 1925. The archway over the goods
entrance may proclaim the old GCR but
the waggons parked inside the goods
entrance tell a different story. *(ROLLR)*

Arthur Wakerley JP (1862–1931) lays the foundation stone for the new council houses he had designed, in 1922. A former mayor of Leicester, Wakerley was an accomplished architect responsible for several significant buildings in Leicester, such as the Turkey Café (1901) and Singer Building (1902) as well as the North Evington suburb. His philanthropic and political ideals were combined with his practical skills when he turned to the design of new council houses: the homes 'fit for heroes' returned from the war. *(ROLLR)*

One of the Wakerley-designed council houses in Green Lane, opened in 1923. Such a house cost £299 to build and was intended as an answer to severe housing shortages after the First World War. The rent was 12*s* 6*d* a week. The design was to be adopted by other housing committees, as far afield as Glasgow and Belfast. *(ROLLR)*

Above: Winston Churchill canvassing in Leicester in 1923. He stood as the Liberal candidate in West Leicester against the Labour candidate, Frederick Pethick Lawrence, and was expected by many to win with ease. The contest was watched with interest around the country, but in the event Churchill lost by over four thousand votes. *(ROLLR)*

Frederick Pethick Lawrence (1871–1961), the Labour MP for West Leicester, 1923–31. His early career had included social work in the East End of London, ownership of a newspaper in which he advocated the socialist cause, and even a spell of imprisonment in 1912 with his wife Emmeline, for their activities in support of women's suffrage. During the Great War he had been a conscientious objector but this did not seem to hinder his later career. He lost his Parliamentary seat in 1931 when he refused to join MacDonald's National Government. *(ROLLR)*

61

Humberstone Gate in the days before Lewis's department store. Lewis's building so dominated the street that it is still hard to think of the skyline without its tower. How must shoppers have reacted when this scene changed in the 1930s? *(ROLLR)*

Below: This view of a busy Granby Street, in January 1929, proves that traffic congestion (on a moderate scale at least) is by no means a new issue for Leicester. *(ROLLR)*

A wonderfully atmospheric photograph of Humberstone Gate one damp morning in the mid-1920s. In the centre is the City Weighing Machine, with the office of the clerk, Arthur Miles, attached. It is interesting to note the effect of rain and traffic on the road surface. *(ROLLR)*

Royal visitors to the Leicester Agricultural Show on 1 June 1928. The Duke and Duchess of York, later King George VI and Queen Elizabeth, emerge from the luncheon tent on their way to see the sheep dog trials. The newspapers then, as they still do now, referred to the Duchess's 'radiant smile'. *(ROLLR)*

Below: One of two visits made by Edward, Prince of Wales, to Leicester in 1927. He spent time with the British Legion and visited the Liberty Shoe Works. Here he is escorted by (among others) the mayor, Alderman James Thomas, and, wielding his handkerchief, the Duke of Rutland. *(ROLLR)*

Prime Minister J. Ramsay MacDonald on his visit to Leicester in 1929 to receive the Freedom of the City. Beside him is the Lord Mayor, Alderman H. Hand. Few on this occasion chose to dwell on the irony of the situation. In 1918 MacDonald had left Leicester under a cloud, having been heavily defeated as candidate for West Leicester in the General Election that followed the end of the war. Although MacDonald had been an MP for the city since 1906, he had earned great unpopularity for his pacifist beliefs and misgivings about the First World War. On his departure the *Leicester Daily Post* had proclaimed: 'the cancer of pacifism is removed and Leicester stands vindicated to the world'. *(ROLLR)*

Below: A civic procession to the cathedral in 1933 or '34. The Mayor, the ironfounder William Key Billings, heads the line of dignitaries, preceded by the mace bearer, Mr Grewcock, and the mayor's chauffeur, Ernest Guildford. Also in the line is Sir Jonathan North (in beard and top hat). Leicester had become a diocesan bishopric in 1926 and after considerable debate, during which St Margaret's and St Martin's churches were the principal candidates, the latter was chosen as the seat of the new bishop. *(ROLLR)*

A busy, lunchtime crowd throngs Gallowtree Gate,
c. 1920. Just visible is an advertisement for giant
rock, one of the specialities of Noblett's, a Liverpool
company, with shops at 4 Gallowtree Gate and 14a
London Road, sadly no more by the 1930s. *(ROLLR)*

An early example of rescue archaeology, as one of Leicester's few remaining medieval houses is painstakingly dismantled in Highcross Street, with the intention of re-erecting it on the new Crown Hills development. *(ROLLR)*

Below: Labourers of the City Council's Highways Department at work in Carlton Street, *c.* 1930. The nearest shop is that of J.J. Webster, paper, rope and twine merchants, who moved shortly after to Lower Brown Street. *(ROLLR)*

Above: A small court at the rear of Navigation Street and Cope's Cottages, soon to give way to redevelopment as a warehouse. Dominating the scene is one of the two huge gasometers on Lower Thames Street. *(ROLLR)*

A reminder of the living conditions endured in some of Leicester's poorer quarters in the 1930s. This backyard scene, with an outside privy in the foreground, was taken at the rear of Eldon Street prior to slum clearance. During the 1920s and 1930s the City Council cleared around 3,250 dwellings. This site later became part of the Sainsbury's supermarket in Humberstone Gate. *(ROLLR)*

No photographic survey of Leicester's past would be complete without pictures from the Pageant of Leicester and Leicestershire of June 1932. Here are the 'forces of good' from the Corpus Christi Guild procession, which wandered across episode three (set at the beginning of the sixteenth century). The Apostles hold aloft their symbols: St Peter his key, St Bartholomew his knife, St Jude a saw, St Simon a fish and so on. *(ROLLR)*

The forces of darkness arrayed in hell's mouth, also from the Pageant. The little demons clearly had far more fun than the Apostles – but they would, wouldn't they? *(ROLLR)*

On 21 June 1932 the new Charles Street was opened by the Lord Mayor of London. Celebrations included an ox roast, and in the far distance the smoke of the fire can just be discerned. The original Charles Street had been extended north and widened, in the first of what were to be sweeping changes in the road system of Leicester. *(ROLLR)*

Built on Victoria Park, and rivalling Lutyens' war memorial arch in size, this is the huge bonfire, built for the celebration of King George V's Silver Jubilee on 6 May 1935. *(ROLLR)*

A Kirby and West milkman, complete with churn, *c.* 1930. James Kirby had started trading in Leicester as a humble cowkeeper in 1861, but by 1868 he had established the Highfields Dairy in Andover Street (then called Hanover Street). Kirby left in 1900 but the business continued to prosper under the direction of a Mr West. In 1916 the business was taken over by the Smith family, who pioneered milk treatment plants and managed the concern so successfully that by 1933 there had been a tenfold increase in milk sales to 2,500 gallons a day. The company moved to its new premises in Western Boulevard in 1934. Kirby & West still provides a daily delivery to thousands of households in Leicester. *(ROLLR)*

A view of shops on the eastern side of Churchgate (numbers 91–7). The greengrocer's business of G.F. Lister on the left, where the milkcart has been parked, survived into the 1960s. The other buildings, Markham's tea rooms and the boot and shoe shop on the corner of Grabel Street, were demolished in the 1930s. The Leicester Co-operative Printing Society's premises, just visible on the far left, were knocked down to make way for a factory. *(ROLLR)*

The Magazine Gateway, 1920s. Although now in isolation on its own traffic island, in the 1920s the Magazine stood off Southgate Street in a complex of Victorian militia buildings. The medieval building was still the headquarters of Leicester's Territorial Army, the Yeomanry, Royal Artillery, and all but two platoons of the 4th and 5th battalions of the Leicestershire Regiment. *(ROLLR)*

An aerial view of the Clock Tower, one sunny
afternoon in the 1920s. The shops on the Haymarket
show up well but so do the many factories and the
blank walls of the Palace Theatre. The south side of
Belgrave Gate, opposite the theatre, has, of course, all
gone to make way for the Haymarket Development.
(ROLLR)

Above: A group of happy boys bound for a seaside holiday at Mablethorpe, *c.* 1930. The Leicester Poor Boys' and Girls' Summer Camp & Institute was established as a charity in 1897, with the aim of providing underprivileged children with a chance to escape, for a time, the grime of Leicester. Generations of children have enjoyed a stay at what is now known by the rather less intimidating title of Leicester Children's Holiday Home at Mablethorpe, and the charity continues its work today. (*ROLLR*)

Leicester schoolboys come face to face with a tiger on an educational visit to the Museum on New Walk, *c.* 1935. (*ROLLR*)

Santa Claus's headquarters in Market Street, one Christmas in the 1920s. For the rest of the year the building was occupied by H. & A. Bennett's. Best known perhaps for their own brand of brushes, Bennett's clearly expanded under Father Christmas's influence to sell a variety of toys, gifts, and some very reasonably priced bikes, trikes and pedal cars. *(ROLLR)*

Above: A crowd of onlookers watch with interest as the last girder of the old railway bridge on the Narborough Road is removed, before construction of the new bridge, 2 September 1928. *(ROLLR)*

A view down Charles Street from Humberstone Gate, *c.* 1930. The area to the right has already been cleared for street-widening and later the construction of Lewis's store. For the time being it is in use as a car park. *(ROLLR)*

The inter-war years were a period of great experimentation on Leicester's roads. Belisha beacons, traffic lights and other inventions came and conquered. Some, however, did not do so well. Experimental rubber bollards appeared in Charles Street but they seemed to have pleased no-one, except perhaps little boys with a mischievous streak. *(ROLLR)*

In 1939 an area around Abbey Street was cleared for the erection of a new bus station to be known as St Margaret's. This was the last act in the redevelopment of Leicester before the Second World War intervened. *(ROLLR)*

Leicester Parks Department workmen astride a rocking horse in Humberstone Park, 1931. The snapshot was taken by their foreman, G. Hollis – so all was above board – and shows, not Sleepy, Happy, Sneezy, Doc and the others, but A. Oldacre, G. Lain, E. Watsize, F. Hastings, F. Bett, B. Bray and B. Mansfield. *(ROLLR)*

Below: A grey, misty view over Leicester, probably from the tower of the Town Hall. The market is packed and there are crowds down both sides of Cheapside. *(ROLLR)*

Blacked-out and Blitzed

Preparations for war . . . a workman paints over the lights of a traffic
bollard in front of the Police Station in Charles Street, in anticipation of
black-out regulations, 1938. *(ROLLR)*

Roy Hill inscribes
the date stone of the
Mantle Road School
air-raid shelters,
built by the staff and
pupils as a lesson in
both bricklaying and
community spirit:
Shelter, built by the
staff and boys, 1939.
E. Chatwin,
headmaster'. *(ROLLR)*

It must have been disconcerting for the onlookers, watching the first preparations against enemy air attack, as police and council workmen set about building a barrier of sandbags outside the police station in Charles Street, 1939. *(ROLLR)*

Above: Civil defence workers and residents of Jervis Street join together for a public anti-gas exercise. Veterans of the Great War must have known the horror of gas as a weapon. Thankfully, although Leicester was bombed, gas was never used. *(ROLLR)*

As early as January 1938 Leicester held a rehearsal for its air-raid precautions. Here two council workmen practise dealing with liquefied gas, carrying in a cannister the solution used to neutralise the gas. An optimistic newspaperman cheerfully reported that the masks caused little discomfort apart from getting 'a bit warm'. *(ROLLR)*

A striking use of camouflage on the cooling towers of the Aylestone Road power station, August 1939. Would the Luftwaffe mistake these concrete monsters for a grove of trees? *(ROLLR)*

Leicester was lucky enough to escape the worst of the blitz but even so there were civilian casualties. In August 1940 the first fatalities occured in Cavendish Road, pictured here with the gas main still burning. Six people were killed and twenty-four injured by the bombs of a single – probably lost – German aircraft. *(ROLLR)*

Leicester's worst air-raid occured on the night of 19 November 1940, the same week that Coventry suffered its devastating attack. Ninety-six people died in the city that night, among them two families (including a six-year-old boy) who were sheltering in the Shoe Mercers Shelter, Peel Street. In this view of Highfield Street and Severn Street, the wreckage of a trailer ambulance litters the foreground, while behind, the contents of a shattered bedroom spill forth. Other buildings gutted included Faire Brothers' premises in Rutland Street and Arthur Kemp's Dover Street works. *(ROLLR)*

Police Constable Alfred Frederick Collins on point duty in Gallowtree Gate on the second day of the Second World War, 4 September 1939. His cloth helmet has given way to a steel helmet and he carries his gas mask over his shoulder. PC Collins joined the Leicester Police on 11 November 1914 and retired, with a full pension, on 1 January 1946. *(ROLLR)*

A parade in honour of the twenty-eight countries united in the struggle against the Axis Powers, held in Victoria Park, 14 June 1942. On the platform the Lord Mayor (Miss Frisby), the Bishop of Leicester and Captain Fouquies of the Free French, accompanied by other dignitaries, took the salute as representatives of the army, civil defence, cadets and other youth organisations marched past. (*ROLLR*)

Members of the Women's Land Army smile for the camera at a rally held in Victoria Park, *c.* 1943. Little – except perhaps the corduroy breeches – of the Land Army girl's lot was enviable. Although their work in agriculture was absolutely vital in ensuring the nation's food supply, it involved long hours, hard labour and conditions of service which were far inferior to those enjoyed by women in the forces. Even after the war the girls were denied many of the benefits granted to civil defence workers. Recognition for their achievements came only very slowly. It was only in the year 2000 that Land Army girls were at last permitted to parade at the Cenotaph. (*ROLLR*)

Above: German prisoners-of-war are marched through Leicester under the watchful eye of a British soldier, *c.* 1945. Many hundreds of German and Italian prisoners worked on farms or civil engineering schemes around Leicester, some of them having to wait years before repatriation. *(ROLLR)*

Victory at last! Rejoicing crowds, lining London Road, watch as a Sherman tank, followed by a Churchill, rumble past them on their way into Leicester for the celebration of victory, 1945. *(ROLLR)*

Recovery and Growth

A view of the High Street from the Clock Tower, *c.* 1955.
The greatest changes in this area since the photograph was taken have
happened behind the scenes. The façades of John Manners, clothiers,
Gilbeys and Fosters, both wine merchants, Lloyds Bank and the other
shops on the northern side of the High Street may have survived
relatively unscathed today, but they have all given way inside to the Shires
development. *(ROLLR)*

On 30 October 1946 King George VI, escorted by Major F.M. Bishop, inspected a guard of honour of the Leicestershire Regiment. A month later, on 28 November, the King honoured the regiment with the title of the Royal Leicestershire Regiment. *(ROLLR)*

The Clock Tower, shortly before the disappearance of trams in 1949. How many hours must Leicester people have spent waiting at the Clock Tower? The perfect rendezvous; so many tram routes and an unmistakable landmark for strangers. Uniforms give this view a wartime feel, though only two are military – the ATS girl beneath the statue of Simon de Montfort and the passing RAF man. The other uniforms at the Tower are those of two tramway employees. *(ROLLR)*

Moving into newly built steel houses on Battersbee Walk, New Parks Estate, *c.* 1949. Leicester City Council's response, like many authorities faced with a housing shortage after the Second World War, was to build simply and swiftly. On the New Parks the boast was that 162 houses were built in as many days. *(ROLLR)*

Dr Charles Killick Millard (1870–1952), former Medical Officer of Health for Leicester, celebrated his eightieth birthday with a ride on his new BSA Bantam motorcycle. Inevitably asked his recipe for such fitness in old age, the doctor attributed it to his life-long abstinence from strong drink and tobacco. *(ROLLR)*

In common with millions of others, the inhabitants of Muriel Road celebrated the coronation of Elizabeth II in 1953 with a street party. For many the dawn of a new Elizabethan age seemed a chance to turn their backs once and for all on the austerity of the postwar years. *(ROLLR)*

Above: The demolition of the temporary war memorial on Town Hall Square, May 1954. The memorial, designed by S. Perkins Pick and B.J. Fletcher, the headmaster of the Art School, had been unveiled on 28 June 1917. The wings of the memorial – one of which has already gone in this view – bore the inscription 'They did not fail us: we must not fail them'. Already en from Leicester and Leicestershire. At the time of demolition the temporary memorial had long been replaced by Lutyens' Arch of Remembrance in Victoria Park. *(ROLLR)*

A demonstration allotment on Town Hall Square, *c.* 1950. Wartime food shortages and the austerity of the immediate postwar period created a desperate need for Britain to feed herself. How better to show how it could be done than a plot in the heart of the city? The city centre allotment remained in front of the Town Hall until 1951. *(ROLLR)*

A picturesque traffic jam in London Road, as part of the
celebrations for the opening of the Newarke Houses Museum
in 1953. The museum building in The Newarke had been
badly damaged by enemy action in November 1940. *(ROLLR)*

Possibly the first Mayor of Leicester to travel by Leicester Corporation horse-power since 1904 when electric trams were introduced, Charles Keene sets out to perform the opening ceremony at Newarke Houses Museum. Once there, the Mayor not only opened the museum but in its garden he unveiled the old High Cross which had been preserved and re-erected. The High Cross was returned to the Market Place in 1976. *(ROLLR)*

A caterpillar of tiny tots from the day nursery run by Foister, Clay and Ward, hosiery manufacturers of Frog Island and Great Central Street, crosses the road en route to the swings in Abbey Park Recreation Ground. The increasing number of working mothers and subsequent demand for childcare were to become ever more important during the the second half of the century. *(ROLLR)*

A hint of what lay in the future for Leicester motorists in August 1954, as resurfacing work in Belgrave Gate causes a tail-back into the city centre. (ROLLR)

Above: Morley's draper's shop at 14 Cheapside, late 1950s. Whether you required fabric for the latest fashions, material for curtains, or yards of mourning crêpe, Morley's was the place to go. *(ROLLR)*

The menswear department of the old Adderly's shop in Market Place and Gallowtree Gate, known by the 1950s as Marshall and Snelgrove (Adderly & Co. Ltd) which advertised itself as 'Departmental store, ladies hairdressers, funeral undertakers and restaurant proprieters. Telegraph address: Adderly, Leicester. Telephone number 5153'. *(ROLLR)*

The tower of Lewis's store in Humberstone Gate, built in 1935–6, was already well established as a landmark on the Leicester skyline when this photograph was taken in about 1950. Although hardly beautiful, the tower was nevertheless survived the demolition of the store and subsequent redevelopment in the 1990s. *(ROLLR)*

Though some of the most important buildings remain – the Magazine and Newarke Houses Museum for example – this view of The Newarke was changed almost beyond recognition in 1966 when the Southgates underpass and dual carriageway were built. When this photograph was taken, on 14 March 1960, the buses still stopped at the shelter and the Territorial Army Centre still stood on Magazine Square. Sometimes, it seems, the price of progress is excessive. *(ROLLR)*

Looking down Bonner's Lane from Oxford Street, prior to demolition of the buildings in 1957. On the corner is the greengrocer's shop of Arthur Parr which was established seventy-five years before. Opposite are the offices of S. Rowsell & Co. Ltd, boot and shoe manufacturers, which still stand today. This area is now dominated by De Montfort University, the former Leicester Polytechnic. *(ROLLR)*

The Birmingham & Midland Motor Omnibus Company's depot on Southgate Street, *c.* 1955. From here buses and Midland Red coaches carried passengers all over the Midlands. The bus station survived the redevelopment of the Southgates area, though its ownership changed first to Midland Fox and then to Arriva Fox County buses. *(ROLLR)*

A view of the Market Place, *c.* 1950, which has changed little apart from the various styles of roofing that have been placed over the stalls. In the distance are the premises of Simkin and James, a department store selling groceries, cheese and wines, next to the Royal Hotel, both of which closed in 1971 to make way for modernisation schemes. *(ROLLR)*

The scene of a car accident on the junction between Fosse Road South and Upperton Road, *c.* 1955. The problems of congested motor traffic were only just beginning. . . . *(ROLLR)*

Peace and quiet at the heart of the city, *c.* 1950. Seemingly far away from worries over traffic, fishermen sit, almost lost in the mist, beside the canalised River Soar just below the Mill Lane Bridge. *(ROLLR)*

Making the
Modern City

In his report published in 1968 Konrad Smigielski, Leicester City
Council's Chief Planning Officer, who had established the city's
first separate planning department in 1962, set out his long-term
objectives for Leicester and described the schemes already underway.
Smigielski, however, was never to see his plans completed, as he left
the city in 1972 after a dispute with councillors. The cover of the
report showed Smigielski's vision of a Clock Tower surrounded by
concrete tower blocks and elevated walkways. *(ROLLR)*

A motorist's view of the Clock Tower, approaching from the High Street, *c.* 1960. To the left, on the corner of New Bond Street, is the shop of Phillips Furnishing Stores Ltd, soon to become Hardy and Company. On the right can be seen the awning of Lennards Footwear. A policeman would not have dared stand here by the late 1990s! Ahead are the buildings demolished in 1966 to make way for the Littlewoods Department Store. *(ROLLR)*

One of the futuristic illustrations in Smigielski's book depicts a monorail stop in Charles Street with an elevated walkway to the Clock Tower. Inspired by an example in Seattle, Smigielski had wanted a monorail to run through the city from Beaumont Leys to Wigston. Dismissed at the time as science fiction, the aim to encourage visitors out of their cars does not seem so far fetched today. *(ROLLR)*

The installation of traffic lights at the junction of Fosse Road North and the A50, July 1964. *(ROLLR)*

A heavy goods locomotive clanks in reverse across the Fosse Lane level crossing on 25 March 1966. The old Great Central Railway, although the newest and one of the best engineered of Britain's main lines, tragically had only a few more weeks of active life left. *(ROLLR)*

A sight to make the mouth water! This interior view of Joblin's sweetshop at 253 Charnwood Street shows Hilda and Gordon Breckon with their daughter Barbara in 1963. Can you remember when a packet of Polos cost 2½d, or a packet of Maltesers 6d? *(ROLLR)*

An interior view of Civil's supermarket on Charnwood Street, *c.* 1962. The supermarket was a new concept which was eventually to revolutionise shopping habits. *(ROLLR)*

The Market Place, *c.* 1970. The strange 'chocolate bar' effect of the market canopy certainly created the modernistic appearance so beloved of planning officers. It was never really accepted by shoppers or stall-holders, however, and lasted only about twenty years. The new roof of the 1990s restored light to the centre of the market. *(ROLLR)*

The devastation of a city. The two features dominating this aerial view of west Leicester in 1966, the forlorn island station of the Great Central Railway and the vast St Nicholas Circle roundabout, symbolise the triumph of the motor car. Seen as inevitable in the 1960s, the dominance of petrol was in question by the end of the century. *(ROLLR)*

The St Nicholas Underpass under construction, 30 December 1966. How many motorists have driven into (and out of) this great chasm since the photograph was taken? St Nicholas's church, already beginning to seem isolated and out of place, stands in the background. *(ROLLR)*

Harvey Lane, Leicester, May 1968. The redevelopers are closing in upon William Carey's Cottage which, like St Nicholas's church in the last photograph, is already looking friendless and alone in a builders' wasteland. *(ROLLR)*

Another hole in the centre of Leicester, 9 February 1966. This time the hole is the site of Littlewood's store in the Haymarket. *(ROLLR)*

The finished product! The great Neapolitan ice-cream slab of Littlewood's, attempting to hide behind the Clock Tower, in May 1968. It is interesting to note how quiet the traffic still was in the late 1960s. *(ROLLR)*

An interested crowd watches as one of the last girder spans is lowered into place on the St Augustine Road bridge, 23 August 1970. The bridge carries the A47, the main route into the city from the west, over the Grand Union Canal. *(ROLLR)*

Waterloo Way under construction, 3 March 1976. The new dual carriageway seems to lead straight to the London Road station. To the left is the church of St John the Divine, soon to be declared redundant and, by the late 1980s, sold off for subdivision into flats. *(ROLLR)*

111

Colourful narrowboats line the towpath in Abbey Park on the occasion of the National Rally of Boats, held from 28 July to 1 August 1967. The Inland Waterways Association which had organised the rally was pessimistic about the future of canals, and chose Leicester because they suspected that the Grand Union Canal might be the next canal to come under threat of closure. They had witnessed a dramatic decline in trading boats on the canals since the first rally in 1950 and feared the government would allow the canal system to fall into disuse. Fortunately such large boat rallies and the work of enthusiasts did succeed in raising the profile of the canals, and preserving what are now recognised to be features of great environmental importance and a highly valued leisure resource. *(ROLLR)*

A horse-bus of the Leicester Corporation's Tramways receives an airing for the Lord Mayor's Show, 2 June 1973. In the background is the YMCA hostel and theatre on East Street. *(ROLLR)*

Of all the writers associated with Leicester, Sue Townsend is probably the most loyal to her native city. Having left school at fifteen she undertook a variety of unskilled jobs until, having joined a writers' group run by the Phoenix Theatre, she was set upon a new path as an author. Her most famous work – *The Secret Diary of Adrian Mole Aged 13¾*, which was first published in 1982, was an outstanding success, particularly after radio broadcasts of readings. Several sequels about the adolescence and subsequent career of Adrian Mole have also been bestsellers. *(ROLLR)*

Simon Schatzberger and Sara McGlasson as Adrian Mole and Pandora in the Phoenix Art Centre's highly popular stage production of *The Secret Diary of Adrian Mole*, 1984, which later went to the West End. Leicester City Council had opened the Phoenix Theatre in 1967 as a temporary arena while the Haymarket Theatre was under construction. However, the Phoenix proved so successful that it continued into the 1980s, producing first-rate drama until cuts in funding brought about its sad demise as a repertory theatre. *(ROLLR)*

The white hell they called Welford Place! A blizzard holds up the traffic at the junction of Welford Place and Welford Road in January 1987. *(ROLLR)*

'Push of Pike' in The Newarke, 1995. The notorious sack of Leicester by the army of King Charles I is re-enacted on its 350th anniversary. In 1645 the town's Parliamentarian garrison refused to open the gates to the Royalist army and so Leicester was first bombarded and then stormed. The citizens paid a heavy price in lives and property for their defiance. The commemoration was slightly less destructive and bloody. (*ROLLR/D. James*)

Opposite: Work commences on the new shopping centre to be opened as The Shires in 1991. With rather more sensitivity than previous developers, the architects sought to create a building which blended in with the Edwardian buildings of the High Street on the exterior, while inside they created a light, airy shopping centre dominated by Egyptian-style columns. (*ROLLR*)

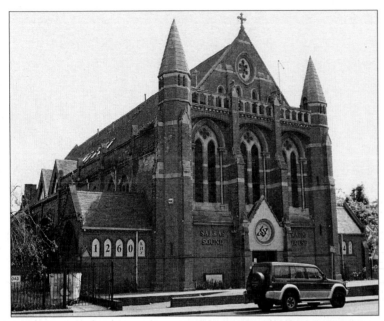

The former Anglican church of St Michael and All Angels (built 1885–7) was bought by the Asian radio station Sabras in 1993. Although Sabras had been broadcasting since 1981 through other commercial stations, they launched their own 24-hour radio station in these premises on 7 September 1995. Situated at the heart of the city's Asian community, the station aimed to broadcast in Hindi, Gujerati, Swahili, Bengali and Cantonese, although news bulletins would be in English – a reflection of Leicester's multi-lingual and multi-cultural society. (*Authors*)

The glamour of Leicester's northern suburbs owes much to its Asian community. The diversity and colour of the Belgrave Road and Melton Road shops draws in customers from throughout the Midlands. Here the Alpa Sweet Mart and posters for the Bollywood Cinema on Melton Road blend in with Edwardian terraced housing. (*Authors*)

The Silver Arcade off Silver Street in the last year of the twentieth century. The arcade was built at the end of the nineteenth century, to the design of Amos Hall. The unspoilt late Victorian elegance of the arcade has benefited from refurbishment and once again adds tone to Leicester's shopping centre. (*Authors*)

A modern view of Horsefair Street, showing how far the city is dominated by traffic. Despite having pioneered the ideas of 'park and ride' and traffic charging, as well as having sacrificed so much for inner and outer ring roads, Leicester is still plagued by the internal combustion engine. (*Authors*)

Leicester has always been remarkably short of public statues but it acquired this new one outside London Road station in 1994. It is in honour of Thomas Cook, the eponymous founder of the world-wide travel agency that still flourishes today. He spent most of his life in Leicester and it was from Leicester that he organised his first railway excursion – a temperance outing to Loughborough in 1841.

It is worthwhile to compare this view of Granby Street now with the view of Granby Street in about 1914, on page 44. What would most surprise the citizens of eighty years ago were they to be whisked forward in time? Casual clothes, perhaps? The telephone kiosk or tower blocks? Possibly the profusion of brightly coloured signs or 'fast' food they advertise? Yet so much has not changed. (*Authors*)

The winding street pattern of medieval Leicester is just discernible in this view of a busy Church Gate. All manner of styles and dates of architecture are visible here from the grand, late-medieval Perpendicular tower of St Margaret's church, to the light, flowing lines of the ultra-modern Shires Centre. (*Authors*)

Below: The interior of the Shires shopping centre. Shoppers are carried up one of the grand escalators, back to their cars in the adjacent multi-storey car park. Below them are two 'decks' of shops, bathed in sunlight from the glass roof, and beside them hang banners celebrating the new Millennium. (*Authors*)

119

The massive tower rises from the site of Leicester's new Space Centre but this Leicester lad has, for a moment, turned his back on progress. He has eyes only for the Abbey Pumping Station and its miniature railway. (*Authors*)

Acknowledgements and Picture Credits

The photographs in this book have all come either from the rich resources of the Record Office for Leicestershire, Leicester and Rutland (ROLLR), and are available for consultation at Long Street, Wigston Magna, Leicester, or from the authors' own collection.

The authors' grateful thanks are due to a number of people, whose help and encouragement have made their task immeasurably easier. The Head of the Leicestershire County Council's Museums, Mrs Heather Broughton, and Chief Archivist, Mr Carl Harrison, both gave encouragement.

We are grateful too to all our colleagues at the Record Office for their assistance and forbearance but Mrs Jan Pearson, whose tireless efforts in obtaining prints of archival photographs, and Mrs Sherry Nesbitt, Mr Mike Raftery, and Mr Keith Ovenden, whose proffered information would otherwise have eluded us, must receive a special mention.

Finally a debt must be acknowledged to the grandparents of our offspring, without whose baby-sitting skills this book would assuredly not have appeared.